Mary Bridges Canedy Slade

The Holiday Concert

Mary Bridges Canedy Slade

The Holiday Concert

ISBN/EAN: 9783337293871

Printed in Europe, USA, Canada, Australia, Japan

Cover: Foto ©Thomas Meinert / pixelio.de

More available books at **www.hansebooks.com**

HOLIDAY CONCERT,

A COLLECTION OF

Dialogues, Recitations, and Concert Exercises,

FOR THE USE OF

SUNDAY-SCHOOL ANNIVERSARIES AND HOLIDAY EXHIBITIONS

BY

MRS. M. B. C. SLADE.

————————

CHICAGO:

PUBLISHED BY

JOHN E. MILLER & CO.

1873.

J. J. SPALDING & CO., Printers. Chicago.

PREFACE.

————•◆•——

The Sunday - School Concert, or Children's Evening, has become a regularly established institution in nearly all churches of the various denominations.

A demand is thus created for such exercises as combine genial, cheerful, and healthful entertainment with useful instruction.

It has been our aim, in this little book, to aid in supplying this demand.

We have also given special attention to the approaching holidays and festivals of Christmas and New Year.

If our work wins the welcome that it has earnestly sought to deserve, it may be followed by others of similar character.

Mrs. M. B. C. SLADE.

Fall River, Mass., Nov., 1872.

The Holiday Concert.

A TALK ABOUT PALESTINE.

WITH MAP UPON THE BLACKBOARD.

BY MINNIE B. SLADE.

Leila. Girls, let us talk a little while about Palestine.

May. Why about Palestine more than any other country?

Leila. Oh, because it is the land where the chosen people of God dwelt, and where the Prophets lived, and where Jesus did his mighty works.

Lizzie. Let us have a map of it. Dora, won't you draw one?

Dora. Why won't *you* draw it yourself?

Lizzie. You draw the outline and I'll put in the Sea of Galilee and the River Jordan.

Leila. And I'll locate some towns.

May. And I can draw some mountains.

(*Dora begins to draw.*)

Ella. Now, while Dora is drawing, let us tell what we know about it.

Dora. Let us give its various names.

Leila. Canaan, Land of Promise, Land of Jehovah, The Holy Land, Judea, Palestine.

Mamie. These are the names of the Land which was promised to Abraham, and where the Children of Israel came after the forty years in the wilderness.

Ella. How large is it?

Leila. One hundred and eighty-five miles long and sixty-five miles wide. Will some one tell us what one of the United States it compares with in size ?

[Let some gentleman in the audience who has been previously requested to do so, say, "It compares in size most nearly with Maryland, though you will see when the map is complete that it is shaped somewhat like New Hampshire.]

Leila. Thank you, Mr.——, we will remember that.

May. Tell us about the trees of Palestine.

Lizzie Here is the olive tree that grows upon the Mount of Olives, and the fig tree, with the stately palm ; and Bashan has its oaks, and Lebanon its cedars.

Mamie. There the sweet white myrtle blooms, and the purple pomegranate, and the air is sweet with roses, and the bright flowers of which our Savior said:

All. "Consider the lilies of the field, how they grow ; they toil not, neither do they spin, and yet I say unto you that even Solomon in all his glory was not arrayed like one of these."

Nora. There is also the rose of Sharon; and I want to tell you that it is not a rose but a narcissus, exactly like the white flowers that we have in the spring. Remember this when you read :

All. "I am the rose of Sharon and the lily of the valley."

Dora. (*Turning from the board.*) I have finished my work. Now while Lizzie draws the Sea of Galilee and the River Jordan, we will talk about the boundaries of Palestine.

Nora. What are those mountains near your northern boundary?

Dora. (*Pointing.*) Those are the Lebanon Mountains, where the great cedars of Lebanon grow.

May. Now show us the eastern boundary.

Dora. (*Pointing to the lines.*) At first, from the north, it passes along by the Mountains of Hermon and Mountains of Gilead ; lower down the River Arnon and the Dead Sea complete the line. Just about here is where Laban said to Jacob :

All. "The Lord be between thee and me, when we are absent one from another."

Dora. And here, near the same place, Jephtha's daughter came out to meet her father with timbrels and dances.

Ella. And what is on the south ?

Dora. It goes from the end of the South Sea to the River of Egypt. And can any one of you tell me what forms the western line ?

Mamie. The Mediterranean, Great, or West Sea.

Lizzie. (*Turning from the board.*) While Leila adds the towns let us talk of the Sea and River.

Mamie. As you have drawn them let us hear you describe them.

Lizzie. The Jordan begins up here in the north, at the springs of Jordan, among the Lebanon Mountains ; it flows south through a lonely country, and enters the Sea of Galilee on the north and leaves it on the south, flowing onward to the Dead Sea.

Ella. I have heard that the waters of the Jordan remain a clear stream, not mingling with the Sea in all its course.

Nora. Can you show us where Jesus came to be baptized by John in Jordan ?

Lizzie. We are not sure, but Bethabara was probably here, a little to the north of Joshua's Passage.

Nora. What was Joshua's Passage ?

May. I will answer you in Scripture words : "Israel came over Jordan on dry land, for the Lord, your God, dried up the waters of Jordan from before you until ye were passed over."

Lizzie. Mr. Blaisdell, may the school sing one verse of "Roll, Jordan Roll," on the 44th page of "Bright Jewels" ?

(*After Singing.*)

Mamie. And now let us talk about the Sea. How large is it ?

Nora. It is ten or twelve miles long.

Lizzie. What are some of the words of Jesus at the sea ?

Ella. He said upon the shore : "Follow me and I will make you fishers of men." He said upon the sea, to the stormy waves : "Peace, be still."

Leila. (*Turning from the board.*) Now, May, while you are plaeing some mountains, I will point out my towns. Please name them. (*Points to north-east shore.*)

Nora. That is one of the Bethsaidas, and Chorazim was near here. (*Points to north-west shore.*)

Dora. That is Capernaum.

(*Points to south-west shore.*)

Ella. That is the other Bethsaida.

Leila. And what are these ?

Lizzie. Tyre on the north, and Sidon on the south.

Mamie. Let me recite what Jesus said of these cities : "Thou, Capernaum, which art exalted unto heaven, shall be brought down to hell : Wo, unto thee, Chorazim, wo, unto thee, Bethsaida ; for if the mighty works had been done in Tyre and Sidon which have been done in you, they had a great while ago repented."

Leila. I point now to Jerusalem, of which Jesus said, "Oh, Jerusalem, Jerusalem, thou that killest the Prophets, how often would I have gathered thy children together even as a hen gathereth her chickens under her wings, but ye would not." And this?

Dora. Is Nazareth, where Jesus was in childhood "subject to his parents."

Leila. And this?

Nora. Bethlehem, where the angels sang "When Jesus was born in Bethlehem of Judea."

Mamie. I wish you could point out just where Jesus said, "Suffer little children to come unto Me."

Lizzie. It is enough for us to know that He said the dear words. I think I would rather feel that He is saying them everywhere. Mr. Blaisdell, may the school sing one verse of "Come Little One," on the 40th page of "Bright Jewels"?

(*After Singing.*)

May. (*Turning from the board.*) I am ready now to point out the mountains. These are?

Leila. The Mountains of Lebanon, where the great cedars grow.

May. And this?

Lizzie. That is Carmel, the only great promontory on the western coast. What prophets loved to come here?

Mamie. It was here that Elijah prayed for rain, till his servant said, "There cometh a little cloud out of the sea like a man's hand."

Dora. I never thought of that before as being from the Mediterranean Sea.

Nora. I suppose the more we search the Scriptures the more things we shall find that we "never thought of before."

Ella. Didn't Elisha also come often to Mt. Carmel?

Mamie. Yes, Elisha was here when the Shunamite woman came to tell him of her dead child. When he said, "Is it well with the child?" and she answered, "It is well."

May. (*Pointing.*) And this is?

Lizzie. That is Mt. Tabor, where Barak and Deborah overthrew the army of Sisera.

Mamie. But we must not linger longer around the Holy Land, though we would gladly tell—

How *Bethlehem* and *Nazareth*,
And sweet *Siloam's Spring*,
And *Kedron* and *Gennesareth*
Their sacred lessons bring :
To *Bethany* would turn our way,
Where Jesus Martha met ;
Or go where oft He went to pray
By night, on *Olivet ;*
But He who made it holy there,
Doth to our spirits tell,
The *Holy Land* is everywhere
Where God with man doth dwell :
And this shall be our willing choice,
Whatever land we see,
His path to tread whose loving voice,
Calls, come and follow Me.

[After this let the school sing " Following Jesus." (pages 10 and 11) from "Starry Crown," by W. O. Perkins. Published by G. O. Russell & Co., Boston. Mass.]

• • •--

OUR TEACHER, GONE HOME.

BY MARY B. C. SLADE.

She dwelt so near her heavenly home,
  No clarion call she needed ;
Death's angel only whispered, "Come ! "
  And glad her spirit heeded.

So like an angel was she here,
  This side the pearly portals,
That we shall surely know her there,
  Among the bright immortals.

Oh, Father, help us loose our hold,
  Our yearning hearts' affection ;
And trust her, in Thine upper fold,
  To Thy dear love's protection!

Following Jesus.

Words by M. B. C. SLADE.

1. Come hith-er, lit-tle child-ren, Oh, will you
2. His foot-prints bright and shin-ing, the way will
3. The sick and weak, and fee-ble, the lame, and
4. The way is ver-y nar-row, the path is
5. So through all paths of du-ty, and do-ing

will you go, Where Je-sus went be-fore you, The
sure-ly show, A-mong the poor and need-y, where
deaf and blind, The lov-ing heart of Je-sus was
ver-y straight, But Je-sus went up thro' it to
good be-low, If you will fol-low Je-sus, you

heavenly way to show? Un-til life's jour-ney's
Je-sus used to go. The poor are al-ways
al-ways sure to find. Oh! swift to help the
find the pearl-y gate, The gold-en street it
by and by, shall go, To dwell with him for-

Following Jesus. — *concluded.*

end - ed, and all its work is done. Oh! will you fol - low
with us, Their doors we can-not shun, If we would fol - low
suff'ring, your lit - tle feet must run. If you would fol - low
en-ters when here our journey's done, Where we shall walk with
ev - er, the best be - lov - ed Son; If you will fol - low

Je - sus the meek and low - ly one? Oh! will you
Je - sus the meek and low - ly one? If we would
Je - sus the meek and low - ly one? If you would
Je - sus the meek and low - ly one? Where we shall
Je - sus the meek and low - ly one? If you will

fol - low Je - sus, the meek and low - ly one.
fol - low, &c.
fol - low, &c.
walk with, &c.
fol - low, &c.

FORBID THEM NOT.

RECITATION FOR A LITTLE BOY.

BY MARY B. C. SLADE.

Sometimes when father comes,
My mother says to me,
" Father is very tired to-night,
Do n't climb upon his knee."

Then father spreads his arms
As wide as they can go,
And takes me up and blesses me,
Because he loves me so.

I think that 's just the way,
And just the reason why
That Jesus used these words to say,
Of children such as I :

"Suffer little children to come unto Me, and forbid them not."
"And He took them up in His arms, put His hand upon them,
and blessed them."—Mark, ix: 14, 16.

WE WOULD SEE JESUS.

BY MARY B. C. SLADE.

First Sch.   We would see Jesus, the wonderful child ;
Second Sch. Go find Him with Mary, His mother so mild,
                In the manger of Bethlehem.
In Concert. Luke, ii: 16.

Third Sch.   And we would see Jesus, the beautiful son ;
Fourth Sch. To Nazareth hills with His parents He 's gone
                To be subject there unto them.
In Concert. Luke, iii: 51.

Fifth Sch.   Oh, we we would see Jesus, to manhood now grown :
Sixth Sch.   Then come to the desert, where fasting and lone,
                From temptation He turns away.
In Concert. Luke, iv: 12.

Seventh Sch. And we would see Jesus, physician so kind ;

Eighth Sch. Then go where the lame, and the halt, and the blind,
Down before Him the people lay.
In Concert. Matt. ix: 35.

Ninth Sch. Oh, we would see Jesus, where us He may teach ;
Tenth Sch. Then enter the synagogue, there will He preach,
Of the Gospel of Love will tell.
In Concert. Luke, iv: 16.

First Sch. And we would see Jesus in some loving home ;
Second Sch. To Bethany, then, at the eventide come,
Where Martha and Mary dwell.
In Concert. Luke, x: 38, 39.

Third Sch. Oh, we would see Jesus, again and once more ;
Fourth Sch. To Olivet come, when the supper is o'er,
Where He often to pray would go.
In Concert. Matt. xxvi: 30.

Fifth Sch. And we would see Jesus when all these are past :
Sixth Sch. Then come unto Calvary, with Him at last,
Where he dies on the Cross of wo !
In Concert. Luke, xxiii: 33.

Seventh Sch. And shall we see Jesus again, by and by ?
Eighth Sch. Oh, yes, if to walk in His footsteps we try,
We shall go to the Lord we love.
In Concert. Luke, xiv: 3.

Ninth Sch. And say, will He see us and show us His face ?
Tenth Sch. Oh, yes ! He has gone to prepare us a place
In the house of our Father above.
In Concert. Luke, xiv: 2.

A CHAIN OF CHARACTERS.

BY MINNIE B. SLADE.

May. Girls, do you remember a play we once had ? We gave a name of a place, as Boston; and then some one else gave the name of another, beginning with the last letter, N. as Newport. Let us try it with Scripture characters.

Lila. Yes: but let us describe our character first, and another may guess whom we mean, and then describe her hero or heroine.

Ella. I'll begin: He is walking all alone, and looks with much interest on all around him. He sees strange trees and beautiful flowers, and queer animals, but he meets no one in all his walk. I see him a few days later, but not now alone: a beautiful woman is with him, and—

Nora. I see! She is Eve, and is in the Garden of Eden with Adam, whom you have described. I think of a very busy woman. She is preparing to receive a dear friend. By and by He comes, and she, though very glad to see Him, goes on with her work, and even tries to get her sister, who is listening to the words of the guest, to help her. But, He says, "Mary hath chosen that good part, which shall not be taken away from her."

Lizzie. Ah, you have told us. It is Martha and Mary; and the guest was Jesus. A—A—Let me think. Oh, I know. The first I know of my hero is, that he went away with his father into a new land, and then, after he was married, he went to Egypt. After some time, he is in another country, pleading with God for the salvation of some cities; but they are so wicked that his pleadings are in vain: and now the Dead Sea covers the site of those cities. Then, afterwards, he goes on such a sad journey. He does n't want to go, but the Lord has told him to take his son, and go up into the mountain. When he gets there, he builds an altar, and his little son asks him: "Behold the fire and the wood, but where is the lamb for the burnt offering?" not knowing that he himself is to be the lamb. For God told his father to sacrifice his son; but just as he is about to kill the boy, he hears God's voice, saying: "Lay not thine hand upon the lad, for now I know that thou fearest God, seeing thou hast not withheld thy son, thine only son from me."

Dora. How glad Abraham must have been that God let his only son Isaac still live! For a word to begin with M, may n't I give the mountain where Isaac was led? Do you know it?

Nora. Mount Moriah, I think. And the only name whose initial is H, that I think of, is a poor slave-woman, who was sent with her son into a desert wilderness, and to whom God said, when she was sad and weeping, "Fear not, for God hath heard."

Dora. The poor woman was Hagar—and I am reminded of the weeping mothers. It is a great many years later, "when Jesus was born in Bethlehem of Judea;" and in the streets of the city are seen cruel soldiers, catching up little children, and killing them, according to the orders of a wicked king; and cries are heard, as of—whom ?

Mamie. "Rachel weeping for her children, and would not be comforted, because they are not." And now listen to my history : A man whom Jesus loved, and who lived not far from Jerusalem, in a home with his sisters. We do not hear much of him till we hear Jesus saying of him, " Our friend sleepeth, but I go that I may awake him out of sleep." When Jesus wakes him, he is all wrapped in white, and comes from a strange sort of a chamber for a man who has been only sleeping.

Lila. Ah ! but that was n't what Jesus meant when he went to call Lazarus from the tomb. He knew that he was dead, but he gave him back his life as easily as he would have waked him if he had just been asleep; just as he raised the little daughter of James, when she slept the sleep of death. And I have to tell of a man whose fame went through all the world. His father said to him as he died: " Know thou the God of thy father, and serve him with a perfect heart and a willing mind; for the Lord searcheth all hearts; " and then he told him of a beautiful work he is to accomplish, when he shall become king. There is so very much to tell of him, that I hardly know what to tell first. He was called upon to judge, and his wisdom was tested in some strange ways. He wrote a beautiful song, or poem, and another book called—

Emma. The Proverbs of Solomon; and I want to tell you one of the stories told of him; not in the Bible, but in the Jewish Talmud. The Queen of Sheba came to him with two wreaths of flowers, and asked him which were natural, and which artificial. The king was in doubt, but saw some bees just outside the window, and had them let in, when, of course, they flew at once to the natural flowers. Then the queen was much surprised that he should think of that way, and as she was going away from him, said: " The one-half of the greatness of thy wisdom was not told me. Blessed be the Lord thy God, which delighted in thee, to set thee upon his throne— "

May. And the beautiful work was the Temple of God, built by Solomon. And I speak of a man who was a ruler among the Jews, whose initial letter is N. He wanted to ask questions once, of one wiser even than Solomon, but did n't dare to be seen doing so, so he came at night. The answers are hard to understand; but he who replies, says: "If I have told you earthly things, and ye believe not, how shall ye believe if I tell you of heavenly things?" And then he said to him these beautiful words: "For God so loved the world, that he gave his only begotten son, that whoever believeth in him should not perish, but have everlasting life." Can you not tell ?

Ella. I think I know. It was Nicodemus who came and said to Jesus: "We know that thou art a teacher come from God, for no man can do these miracles that thou doest, except God be with him." And now, I give one which is hardly fair, for it is the man's first name that begins with S, and he is most frequently called by his last name. He is walking with his brother, by the Sea of Galilee, and is called, with him, from his occupation; and in his usual impetuous way, he hastens to obey. I find him constantly at the head of his companions, speaking for them, active for them. Twice he throws himself into the water, from the ship he is in, eager to meet his master; and I find him, as his master is about to leave him, earnestly promising always to love and acknowledge him; and then, I see him denying all love for him.

Lizzie. I see ! It is Simon Peter. I have thought that he was just the one to write this that is in his epistle: "The Lord is long-suffering to us-ward, not willing that any should perish, but that all should come to repentance." Because he must have been so glad that the Lord came back, after the resurrection, and forgave him, and showed that he was long-suffering to *him-ward*, when he repented so deeply and sorrowfully.

May. If we had time, we would like to tell of the one suggested by Peter's last letter—the beautiful Ruth, gleaning in the field, and caring so tenderly for her mother; then of Haggari, to whom the Lord said: "My spirit remaineth with you; fear not." And then of the grand old prophet, Isaiah, who foretold of our Saviour: "He was wounded for our transgressions; he was bruised for our iniquities." But one name so constantly suggests another, that we can only close by saying we will remember this last letter with which to begin again some other trial.

SIX SCENES IN A NOBLE LIFE.

BY MARY B. C. SLADE.

First Scholar. We show you to-night six scenes—six varied pictures. As we show them, if you recognize the characters and the places, will you raise your hands?—but do not tell us what you think they are, until all the scenes are shown. Our first picture is, THE SCHOLAR.

Second Scholar. In a distant city I see a venerable and learned old man ; near him sits a young man studying from a roll that he holds in his hand, and unrolls as he reads. He is being taught " according to the perfect manner " of his time.

Who is the old man? Raise your *hands*, but not your *voice*. How many know who the young man is ? Let us see more hands. How many know what he is studying ?

First Scholar. Our second picture is, THE CONSENTING WITNESS.

Third Scholar. i must show him to you in a less attractive attitude—I see him standing a willing witness to the death of a good man. He does not soil his own scholarly hands by throwing stones ; but he takes care of the garments of those who are cruelly doing so.

Will all who recognize this scene raise their hands ?

Who is the good man ? What is he called ?

Let *every one* who knows raise his hand.

First Scholar. Our third picture is THE INTERRUPTED JOURNEY.

Fourth Scholar. I show you a startling picture ; things are getting worse and worse with our young man. I see him dashing along the highway leading to an ancient city. His heart is full of hate and his voice full of threatenings. Suddenly, at noon, in the light of mid-day, a bright light shines over him, and a voice says— What ? How many know ? Now, he falls to the ground and gropes as though in blindness. Who is he ? *Raise only your hands.* Let us see *more* hands.

First Scholar. Our fourth picture is A MAN IN A BASKET.

Fifth Scholar. I show you a somewhat comical situation, but one that will rouse your sympathies. It is now more than three years later. At last the young man has come to the same city ; but he is oh, so changed ! What he once hated now he loves. Him whom he once scorned, now he delights to serve. I see the scholarly young man, the enraged persecutor, the stricken traveler, the changed man, in the darkness of night, being let down from an upper window in a basket! Raise your hands if you know, now, *who* he is ? Where he is ? Why he is in this situation ?

First Scholar. Our fifth picture is, THE BEAUTIFUL HILL.

Sixth Scholar. And now, I show a grand picture : He is in a rich and magnificent city. He stands upon a hill, from which he can see lovely islands, in a placid sea. All around are temples, and palaces, heathen statues and idols and altars. He points to one altar with a strange inscription. What is it ? Remember, do not speak ; only raise hands ! What is the hill? What is the city ? How many now know ? We want to see more hands. If our pictures are *good*, you must recognize them.

First Scholar. Our seventh and last is, AN OLD SOLDIER.

Seventh Scholar. Look reverently upon my closing scene. I show you a worn, old soldier ; worn in the service of this Master whom once he hated, but whom he has long loved and served. He is writing a letter to his "beloved son in the faith." This letter was written centuries ago, but I have seen it. Have you ?

Thinking of his past life, and of the end that draws nigh, and of his long warfare, what does he say ? How many know ?

(*The scenes now being all shown, the following questions are asked, and answers drawn from the audience :*)

Second Scholar. Who was the old man in the picture ?

Answer. Gamaliel.

Who was "The Scholar ? "

Answer. Saul of Tarsus.

What was he studying ?

Answer. The Jewish law.

Third Scholar. What is the scene of my cruel picture of "The Consenting Witness ? "

Answer. The death of Stephen.

At whose feet did the wicked men leave their clothing ?

Answer. At Saul's feet.

Fourth Scholar. In "The Interrupted Journey," where was Saul going ?

Answer. To Damascus.

For what was he going ?

Answer. To persecute the Christians.

What were the words he heard ?

Answer. Saul, Saul, why persecutest thou me ?

Fifth Scholar. In my picture of " The Man in the Basket," where is he ?

Answer. In Damascus.

What had he been doing ?

Answer. Preaching the gospel.

Why let down in a basket ?

Answer. To escape from his enemies.

Sixth Scholar. Where was " The Beautiful Hill ? "

Answer. In Athens.

What was it ?

Answer. Mars Hill.

Who is preaching there ?

Answer. St. Paul.

What is the inscription upon the altar ?

Answer. To the Unknown God.

Seventh Scholar. Who is my "Old Soldier ? "

Answer. The Apostle Paul.

To whom is he writing his letter ?

Answer. To Timothy.

What does he say ?

All of the class in concert. I have fought the good fight ; I have kept the faith : henceforth there is laid up for me a Crown of Righteousness.

First Scholar Recites.

At the feet of wise Gamaliel he learns the Jewish law ;
At Stephen's death consenting to the cruel deed he saw ;
On the way to far Damascus, struck blind in noon day light :
In Damascus, from his enemies, escaping, in the night ;
On Mars Hill the heathen telling of the wonderful Unknown.
With his warfare well-nigh ended, calmly waiting for his crown ;
These are our varied pictures, and the central form in all,
The Apostle to the Gentiles, God's faithful servant, Paul.

WHERE ARE THE NINE?

A RECITATION FOR FIVE CHILDREN.

BY MARY B. C. SLADE.

Not, as of old, the Blessed One we find,
Healing the lepers, and the lame, and blind,
But His dear Spirit in our hearts is nigh ;
And thus I hear His tender accents cry—
" If ten I call and only one is mine,
  Where are the nine ? "

There were some weary, heavy-laden men,
I counted them and saw that there were ten :
One turned aside to hear that voice, so blest,
That says, " Come unto Me, I give you rest ;
Welcome," says Jesus, " but, oh, son of mine,
  Where are the nine ? "

A band of women saw I, mild and fair,
I counted them and found that ten were there :
One turned aside, and said in accents sweet,
" I chose the better part, at Thy dear feet."
" Welcome," said Jesus, " but, oh, daughter mine,
  Where are the nine ? "

A group of little children gathered round,
I counted them and ten dear lambs I found ;
One turned aside, for, glad and happy, she
Heard, " Let the little children come to me ;
Welcome," said Jesus, " but dear lamb of mine,
  Where are the nine ? "

The one that comes, His arms enfold with love ;
I hear Him calling for the nine that rove
O'er the dark mountains, through the dreary ways ;
His voice is sounding, and it sweetly says,
" I go to seek and save all these of mine ;
  Where are the nine ? "

SACRED WORDS.

FOR TWELVE BOYS.

BY MINNIE B. SLADE.

I.

How we wish, when we read of the old Scripture time,
We might hear now, the sentences sweet and sublime,
Such as given by Peter to men from afar,
At Pentecost. Tell us, please, what his words are.

II.

But Peter, standing up, with the eleven, lifted up his voice, and
said unto them : Ye men of Israel, hear these words. Ye have
taken, and with wicked hands have crucified and slain. This Jesus
hath God raised up, whereof we all are witnesses. Therefore, let
all the house of Israel know assuredly, that God hath made that
same Jesus whom ye have crucified, both Lord and Christ.—Acts
ii : 14, 22, 32, 36.

III.

What was said by the Prophet Isaiah, in his word,
Of the Christ, of whose coming the Jews had oft heard,
Where he tells of His bearing the cross for our sake ;
Of His patient submission ; oh, how does he speak ?

IV.

He hath borne our griefs and carried our sorrows ; He was
wounded for our transgressions ; He was oppressed and He was
afflicted, yet He opened not His mouth ; He is brought as a lamb
to the slaughter, and as a sheep before her shearers is dumb, so
He openeth not His mouth ; He hath poured out His soul unto
death, and He was numbered with the transgressors ; and He bare
the sins of many, and made intercession for the transgressors.—
Isaiah, liii : 4, 5, 7, 12.

V.

We would hear our Lord's sermons and listen, as He
Showed His teachings to all, on the Mount by the sea.
Tho' we hear not His voice, we may know how He taught,
And then healed the sick, when so many were brought.

VI.

And seeing the multitude, He taught them, saying :

Ye have heard that it hath been said, Thou shalt love thy neighbor and hate thine enemy. But I say unto you, love your enemies, bless them that curse you, do good to them that hate you, and pray for them which despitefully use you and persecute you.

Ask and it shall be given you ; seek and ye shall find ; knock and it shall be opened unto you. Enter ye in at the strait gate, because strait is the gate and narrow is the way which leadeth unto life.—Matt. v : 1, 43, 44 ; vii : 7, 13.

VII.

To Paul at Mars Hill, we so gladly would go,
Where he taught that the Unknown God all men may know,
Let us listen and hear what he said, as he talked,
While some him believed, but far more only mocked.

VIII.

Then certain philosophers took him and brought him unto Areopagus, saying, "May we know what this new doctrine whereof thou speakest is ?" Then Paul stood in the midst of Mars Hill and said, "Ye men of Athens, as I passed by I found an altar with this inscription : To the Unknown God. Whom, therefore, ye ignorantly worship, Him declare I unto you. God that made the world, seeing that He is Lord of heaven and earth, dwelleth not in temples made with hands. But now commandeth all men everywhere to repent, because He hath appointed a day in the which He will judge the world in righteousness, by that Man whom He hath ordained ; whereof He hath given assurance unto all men, in that He hath raised Him from the dead.—Acts, xvii : 16, 19, 22, 23, 24, 30, 31.

IX.

We would, too, have heard David, who sang God's care
Over all who approach Him in love and in prayer.
Will you tell what he said, in the long, long ago ?
Though his voice long is hushed, yet his words we may know.

X.

I will lift up mine eyes unto the hills from whence cometh my help. My help cometh from the Lord which made Heaven and earth. Behold He that keepeth Israel shall neither slumber nor sleep. The Lord shall preserve thy going out and thy coming in, from this time forth and even forever more.—Psalm, cxxi: 1, 2, 4, 8.

XI.

After John saw the visions, he surely would tell
Of the beauty of Heaven, which he knew so well.
But he left us his record. We tell you the sight
So wondrous with beauty, with God's glory bright.

XII.

And I saw a new heaven and a new earth, for the first heaven and the first earth were passed away ; and there was no more sea. And God shall wipe away all tears from their eyes, and there shall be no more death, neither sorrow nor crying ; neither shall there be any more pain. And there shall be no night there ; and they need no candle, neither light of the sun ; for the Lord God giveth them light.—Rev. xxi : 1, 4 ; xxii : 5.

I'LL NOT TELL.

A CHRISTMAS COLLOQUY FOR TWO, WITH CHORUS.

BY MARY B. C. SLADE.

First.   Oh, what shall you give your father and mother,
  This beautful Christmas day ?
 What gifts shall be for your sister and brother,
  And all of your dear ones, say ?

Second.   I'll not tell, and you will not know,
 Till Christmas trees with their blooms shall glow.
  I'll not tell, I'll not tell !
 But, by and by, when the gifts you see,
 Will you sing the Christmas song with me,
 While the angels sing with us again ?

Angel Cho.   *Peace, peace on earth, good will to men !*
   (*To be sung a little way off.*)

First.   Say, what shall you give the poor little people
  That shivering speed away,
 Through frosty streets, while the chimes in the steeple
  Ring merry for Christmas Day ?

Second.   I'll not tell, and you will not know,
         Till Christmas baskets to find them go !
         I'll not tell, I'll not tell !
         But by and by, when the gifts you see,
         Will you sing the Christmas song with me,
         While the angels sing with us again ?
Angel Cho.   *Peace, peace on earth, good will to men!*

First.   And what shall you give the angel throng,
         Oh, what can you give to them ;
         The shining host that were singing the song
         To the shepherds of Bethlehem ?

Second.   I'll not tell, and you will not know
         Till we give them the song we sing below,
         I'll not tell, I'll not tell !
         But by and by, when the gifts you see,
         Will you sing the Christmas song with me,
         While the angels sing with us again ?
Angel Cho.   *Peace, peace on earth, good will to men!*

First.   And what shall you give the Father in heaven,
         Your kind and your loving Friend?
         All things you have unto you He hath given ;
         What gift unto Him can you send ?

Second.   I will tell, and His eye can see
         That our loving hearts shall His offering be!
         I will tell, I will tell !
         And by and by, when the gifts you see,
         Will you sing the Christmas song with me.
         While the angels sing with us again ?
         Peace, peace on earth, good will to men!

PASSING AWAY—LET THEM PASS.

FOR NEW YEAR'S, OR ANNIVERSARY.

BY MARY B. C. SLADE.

This should be given by *eleven girls*, each holding in her right hand the letters of PASSING AWAY, and in her left those of LET THEM PASS. The letters of each motto should be lifted and held in line, during the recital of the chorus containing it.

First Scholar.   Swift flew the seasons, and the year;
                   Again we haste to gather here;
                   Winter, Spring, Summer, Autumn bright
                   Have onward sped, with rapid flight,
All in Concert. And as they pass, we sadly say—
                   Passing away! Passing away!

Eleventh Scholar. Not sadly—work that Spring begun,
                   Summer and Autumn well have done;
                   They gave us gladness, joy, and mirth;
                   They crowned with loveliness the earth.
All in Concert. So say good-by, and not, alas!
                   Say, let them pass! Yes, let them pass!

Second Scholar. How bright the flowers o'er hill and field!
                   How sweet the perfume that they yield!
                   How sad it seems, the time has come
                   When we must miss their joyous bloom!
All in Concert. And as they pass, we sadly say,
                   Passing away! Passing away!

Tenth Scholar.   Not sadly—there was surely need
                   The flowers should fade, or tiny seed.
                   And ripened fruit, and golden grain
                   Would never bless the earth again,
All in Concert. So say good-by, and not, alas!
                   Say, let them pass! Yes, let them pass!

Third Scholar.   All through the Summer-time, we heard
                   The hum of bee, the song of bird;
                   Now gone is every tuneful sound,
                   From all the silent world around.
All in Concert. And as they pass, we sadly say,
                   Passing away! Passing away!

Ninth Scholar.   Not sadly—they have only flown,
                   To seek some warm and flowery zone;
                   They 'll come when Spring flies home, and then
                   Sing just such merry songs again.
All in Concert. So say good-by, and not, alas!
                   Say, let them pass! Yes, let them pass!

Fourth Scholar.   Here, week by week, the seasons through,
We come, our happy work to do.
And now, we see how quickly flies,
A year of opportunities.

All in Concert.   And as they pass, we sadly say,
Passing away! Passing away!

Eighth Scholar.   Not sadly—though we have not done
All that we might, some sheaves we 've won;
And other days are yet in store,
For sowing, reaping, gleaning more.

All in Concert.   So say good-by, and not, alas!
Say, let them pass! Yes, let them pass!

Fifth Scholar.   We wish that we might ever stay
In youth's bright spring-time, glad and gay;
But swiftly fade life's sunrise hours;
Its morning sunshine, dewy flowers;

All in Concert.   And as they pass, we sadly say,
Passing away! Passing away!

Seventh Scholar.   Not sadly—there is work to do—
As life goes on, for me and you.
These morning hours, our strength complete,
To bear the burden and the heat.

All in Concert.   So say good-by, and not, alas!
Say, let them pass! Yes, let them pass!

Sixth Scholar.   One year ago! since then have flown,
To far-off mansions, many a one,
So beautiful, so loved, so dear,
Whose happy tones we used to hear.

All in Concert.   And as they pass, we sadly say,
Passing away! Passing away!

Eleventh Scholar.   *Not sadly*—loving kindness flows
Through all that comes, and all that goes—
And, Bless the Lord, we 'll try to say,
For He gives, or takes away!

All in Concert.   So say good-by, and not, alas!
Say, let them pass! Yes, let them pass!

TERMINAL LETTERS—NAMES OF PLACES.

BY MARY B. C. SLADE.

First Scholar. Bethlehem. "Jesus was born in Bethlehem of Judea." *M.*

Second Scholar. Mars Hill. "Paul stood in the midst of Mars Hill." *L.*

Third Scholar. Lebanon. "The cedars of Lebanon which God hath planted." *N.*

Fourth Scholar. Nazareth. Jesus, with his parents, "came to Nazareth, and was subject unto them." *H.*

Fifth Scholar. Horeb. "Elijah went, forty days and forty nights, unto Horeb, the Mount of God." *B.*

Sixth Scholar. Bethesda. "There is, at Jerusalem, a pool called Bethesda." *A.*

Seventh Scholar. Ararat. "And the ark rested upon the mountains of Ararat." *T.*

Eighth Scholar. Tyre. "Hiram came out from Tyre, to see the cities which Solomon had given him." *E.*

Ninth Scholar. Elim. "And they came to Elim, where there were twelve wells of water." *M.*

Tenth Scholar. Moab. "Moses, the servant of the Lord, died then in the land of Moab."

TERMINAL LETTERS—NAMES OF PERSONS.

BY MARY B. C. SLADE.

The use of Terminals, as in "A Chain of Characters," on page 13, may be given in a simple form, as a Class, or Concert Exercise, as follows:

First Scholar. Adam. Father of Cain and Abel. *M.*

Second Scholar. Miriam. Sister of Moses. *M.*

Third Scholar. Marcus. Nephew of Barnabas. *S.*

Fourth Scholar. Sarah. Wife of Abraham. *H.*

Fifth Scholar. Hannah. Mother of Samuel. *H.*

Sixth Scholar. Hagar. Mother of Ishmael. *R.*

Seventh Scholar. Rachel. The wife of Jacob. *L.*
Eighth Scholar. Lot. The nephew of Abraham. *T.*
Ninth Scholar. Tamar. Daughter of David. *R.*
Tenth Scholar. Rebecca. The wife of Isaac. *A.*

This exercise may be continued as long as the limits of the time permit. The interest will constantly increase.

—•♦•—

AWAY, BRIGHT BIRD!

A WINTER RECITATION FOR A LITTLE BOY.

BY MARY B. C. SLADE.

Away, bright bird of the joyous song !
Why linger here in the cold so long ?
There 's a bright, fair land in the southern clime,
Where the warm sun shineth all the time.
Then haste away, ere the cold frosts chill thee,
Or the blasts of the north wind kill thee !

Fear not to cross the raging sea,
But fly along on thy wings so free ;
For He who keepeth thee, on the land,
Holdeth the wave at His command.
Then haste away, ere the cold frosts chill thee,
Or the blasts of the north wind kill thee !

But when the warm spring months again
Bring the sweet south wind and the gentle rain,
And the flowers are blooming wild and wide,
And grass springing up on the green hill-side,
Come again ! we 'll gladly meet thee;
Come again ! with joy we 'll greet thee !

- •♦•--

BLACKBOARD EXERCISE IN SCRIPTURE NAMES.

BY MARY B. C. SLADE.

One scholar stands at the blackboard and asks the questions. As six others, in turn, give the answers, she writes the names, with capitals for both initials and finals, arranging both these in perpendicular lines.

First Scholar. Tell me the waters where the kings from Joshua met their fate.

Second Scholar. Joshua came against them by the waters of *Merom.*—Joshua, xi:7.

First Scholar. Tell me the land Ezekiel said should all be desolate.

Third Scholar. All *Idumea,* even all of it, shall be desolate. —Ezekiel, xxxv:15.

First Scholar. Tell me the rock in the wilderness where Benjamin refuge found.

Fourth Scholar. The men of Benjamin turned and fled to the wilderness, unto the rock *Rimmon.*—Judges, xx:47.

First Scholar. What is the prophet's name who told Abijah's sayings and ways?

Fifth Scholar. The acts of Abijah, and his sayings and his ways, are written in the story of the prophet *Iddo.*—Second Chronicles, xiii:22.

First Scholar. What was the name of the prophetess old, in the temple who spent her days?

Sixth Scholar. There was one *Anna,* a prophetess, who departed not from the temple.—Luke, ii:36.

First Scholar. What is the place where Laban said the beautiful words, "so sweet, that we love to recall when we part from friends, and say till again we meet"?

Seventh Scholar. *Mizpah.* For Laban said, The Lord watch between me and thee, when we are absent one from another.—Genesis, xxxi:49.

First Scholar. Now read the initials of all our words, and see if you know the name.

All in Concert. *Miriam,* sister of Moses, who with him from Egypt came.

First Scholar. Now read the terminals of the word, and tell me the name, if you can.

All in Concert. *Manoah,* the father of Samson, the strong and the mighty man.

SUFFER LITTLE CHILDREN.

FOR MISSIONARY CONCERT.

BY MINNIE B. SLADE.

I.

Jesus loves the little children,
For He said, one day,
"Let the children come to me—
Keep them not away."

II.

There are many little children
Who have never heard
Of His love and tenderness—
Of His Holy Word.

III.

I would tell those little children,
If they all could hear,
How He spoke to His disciples,
With the children near.

IV.

Listen, now, while we repeat it :
Hark ! 't is very sweet !
I should think 't would make the children
Hasten Him to meet.

ALL.

" Suffer little children to come unto me, and forbid them not,
for of such is the Kingdom of Heaven."

———•+•———

JAIRUS' DAUGHTER.

BY MARY B. C. SLADE.

She slept the sleep of death;
And the free limbs, that late so buoyant sprang,
And the red lips, whence joyous accents rang,
Were stilled.   The morning's breath

Played o'er the sleeper's brow,
Smooth as the polished marble; and as white
As on the lily's cheek the morning's light;
And pure as clustered snow.
But, from the eyes' closed lid
Flashes no ray to tell the soul is there;
The casket still is precious, and so fair—
Where is the bright gem hid ?
Then, to that home of death,
Came Jesus, with His faithful witness-band,
And to the weeping ones that round her stand,
"She is not dead !" he saith.
He called her by her name;
She heard the voice that said, "Damsel, arise !"
Strength thrilled her feet, and light illumed her eyes—
Again her spirit came.
Whence came the maiden, then ?
We only know that when she heard his voice,
And felt his touch, with glad and willing choice,
Her spirit came again.

———•✦•———

GLAD NEW YEAR.

BY MARY B. C. SLADE.

PERSONS:

Old Year; New Year; Seasons; Months; Fairies.

COSTUMES:

These may be copied from pictures familiar to every one,
making a special effort to use every means to render them
symbolical. The Fairies' wings may be made of gauze, drawn over
a wire frame. The throne should be in front of a screen of
evergreen, from behind which the various characters enter.

(*The two Fairies come in, and find the Old Year dozing upon his
throne. They clap their hands and laugh, very gently.*)

First Fairy.   Ha! ha! ha! what a funny sight, I hardly can believe,
The Old Year is fast asleep, upon glad New Year's
Eve.

Second Fairy (climbing up behind the throne, and tickling his ear with a straw).

I'll rouse the sleepy fellow, if I can reach his ear.
Wake up! wake up! 'tis New Year's Eve, and she
will soon be here.

Old Year (rising, and slowly descending the throne).

Ah, yes, I must be going; my last swift moments fly;
The old pass out, the new come in, the changes
hurry by.
My work is done; with willing steps, I peaceful pass
away,
In hope that I have blessed and served earth's
children in my stay.
In hope that I have nearer brought the time when
sin shall cease,
And angels in the air again shall sing the songs of
peace.
I wish that I could hear the song before I pass away—
The angel song of promise I heard on happy
Christmas Day.

*(Voices behind the screen sing the first stanza of " Praises " from Mrs.
Miller's " Christmas Carols.")*

Old Year.   And now, I go ; as on the ear those last sweet echoes
swell,
I hear the New Year's coming chimes, the Old
Year's passing bell.

Old Year (to First Fairy).

Give fair New Year my golden crown *(to second Fairy)*
my royal scepter bright,
And lead her to the throne I leave—good-by, good-
will, good-night.

*(Old Year goes out very slowly.   As the bell stops ringing, let the voices
sing first stanza of " Ring Out Merry Bells," from Mrs. Miller's
" Christmas Carols.")*

*(New Year enters very gaily.   The Fairies go to meet her, with crown
and scepter).*

New Year.   What bright, new scene is this, and what is here?
First Fairy.   This is thine earthly throne, O, glad New Year.
                                        (Leads her to it.)

New Year.   And who is he who has so sadly gone?
Second Fairy. The gray Old Year; he left for thee his crown.
                                  (*Crowns her.*)
New Year.   What hast thou in thy hand, sweet fairy, tell.
Second Fairy. This is thy scepter; wisely rule, and well.
New Year.   A throne, a crown, a scepter—and are ye ··
              All of the subjects that belong to me?
Fairies.   Ah, no; here hastes a gay and merry throng;
              Four happy Seasons come, with laugh and song.
(*The Seasons enter.*)
First Fairy (*presenting Spring*).
              This, royal lady, is the merry Spring.
Second Fairy (*presenting Summer*).
              And this, the Summer-time, so fair, so bright.
First Fairy (*presenting Autumn*).
              This is the brown-cheeked Autumn that I bring.
Second Fairy (*presenting Winter*).
              And this, brave Winter, in her garments white.
Seasons (*in Concert*).
              O, beautiful New Year,
              Thy loyal servants we;
              Each in her own bright sphere
              Will minister to thee.
              As we our gifts bestow,
              Our varied treasures, rare,
              Thy stores shall overflow,
              On New Year, bright and fair;
              And each of us has daughters three,
              Who joyfully will wait on thee.

The Fairies (*leading in March, April, and May*).
              Make way! Make way!
              Here come March, April, May.
Spring.   These are the children of the Spring,
              Glad service now to you they bring.
March (*bowing before the New Year*).
              I'm a wild young maiden;
              And winter's ways I follow;
              With chill, rough winds, snow-laden,
              I sweep o'er hill and hollow.

April (bowing before the New Year).

> And when, with-her rousing rally,
> Her voice has wakened the flowers,
> I, over the hill and valley,
> Will woo them with gentle showers.

May (bowing).　And I, O, then, I will bring them
> The buds and the blossoms dear,
> And over the wild woods fling them,
> To gladden the bright New Year.

The Fairies (leading in June, July, and August).

> Make room! make room! in glorious prime,
> Come the daughters fair of Summer-time.

Summer.　My daughters three at thy feet shall bow,
> And offer their loyal service, now.

June (to the New Year).

> Roses red and hawthorn white,
> Blue of heaven, and gold of sea,
> Songs of birds, green fields so bright,
> Perfect gifts, June offers thee.

July (to New Year).

> I the glorious day will bring,
> When the freedom bells shall ring;
> Brighter green shall deck the hills,
> Deeper blue the sky and rills.

August (to New Year).

> I will spread, o'er field and plain,
> Billowy seas of golden grain.
> Maidens fair my songs shall sing,
> As the harvest home they bring.

Fairies (with August, September, and October).

> Another stately three are here:
> We lead them to thee, glad New Year.

Autumn.　My noble daughters, New Year, see,
> What treasures they will offer thee!

September (to New Year).

> I'll bring for thee my clusters of the vine,
> And golden corn, and glowing fruits of mine.

October (to New Year).

    I'll bring thee brown nuts, from the wind-tossed
        bough,
    And bright-hued forest leaves to deck thy brow.

November (to New Year).

    My cheery days shall crown thy perfect prime,
    With the glad season of thanksgiving time.

Fairies (with December, January, and February).

    Make room for these to enter in thy train:
    Three last bright links that make thy perfect chain.

Winter.

    Brave, strong, and hardy are my daughters here;
    They offer faithful service, Oh, New Year!

December.

    Stern, cold, and hard I seem, no flowers I bring;
    Nor birds, their soft, sweet, summer songs to sing;
    But one glad, glorious time, I bring along—
    The Christmas time, and the old Christmas song.

*(All now on the stage sing first stanza of Mrs. Miller's "Christmas
Carols.")*

January.

    And I the honor have, O lovely Queen,
    To usher in each happy New Year scene;
    The bright young months that 'round thee gaily
        speed,
    I have the honor and the joy to lead.

February.

    And I, my gladdest service is to say,
    With me the reign of storms shall pass away;
    The richest gift I offer, is to bring
    Close in my train, the ever-welcome Spring.

All (joining hands, and going around the throne).

    And so around the New Year's throne, her happy
        subjects go.

New Year.   So I the loyal service take my subjects all bestow.

All.   So is our New Year's fresh young life, with song
    and dance begun.

New Year.   So will we seek to bless the earth, until our course
    is run.

All.   And as we onward, onward haste, and circle 'round
    the year,

New Year (*rising and extending her scepter*).

  May light and love and joy and peace descend and
  bless us here.

Closing Tableaux. At this point, let the New Year stand, with
extended scepter; the Months and Seasons in graceful attitudes,
while the Fairies shall have led the Old Year just to the threshold,
where he stands, with his hand extended, as in parting blessing.
The curtain may then fall, for a change of positions, and another
tableau be presented, with New Year seated, and the Months and
Seasons in four groups.

THE WALK TO EMMAUS.

SUNDAY-SCHOOL CONCERT RECITATION.

BY MARY B. C. SLADE.

[Let the class recite, in turn, Luke xxiv: 13, 17, 28, 32.   One scholar
recites the poem.]

As, walking from Jerusalem,
 Two sad disciples went,
Jesus drew nigh and talked with them,
 Till day was now far spent.

But, while their hearts within them burned,
 Their holden eyes were dim;
And, though they loved Him as they learned,
 A stranger thought they Him.

As they drew nigh to Emmaus,
 Toward eve, He made as though
He would not end his journey thus,
 But farther onward go.

"Abide with us," to Him they said;
 Then, at the hallowed board,
In breaking of the evening bread,
 Knew their beloved Lord.

With holden eyes, along thy way,
The Lord dost thou not know ?
Constrain Him, that He with thee stay,
Nor farther onward go.

And, when He tarrieth with thee,
The evening board to grace,
Thine opened eyes with joy shall see
And know His blessed face.

MR. VERY'S SERMON,

A RECITATION FOR A BOY.

BY MARY B. C. SLADE.

I shall speak very briefly, dear ladies, and dear sirs;
My speech it will be chiefly unto the ministers.
Mr. Very preached a sermon, and I can't tell you next,
What was Mr Very's subject, nor Mr. Very's text.
But a lady hastened to him, as on the steps he stood,
With, " Oh, dear, Mr. Very, your sermon was *so* good !
I have n't heard a sermon, in how long I can't tell,
That pleased me, Mr. Very, and suited me *so* well!"
Mr. Very was delighted, for sugar plums are sweet,
And such nice sugar plums of praise, who would n't like to eat?
So he thanked the lady, kindly, and said that he was glad;
He hoped to preach acceptably, and he rejoiced he had.
Then asked her why his sermon so excellent she thought.
" Oh! I liked it, Mr. Very, *because it was so short !* "

THE BIRTH OF JESUS.

Recitation. The birth of Jesus Christ was on this wise: Joseph
went up from Galilee, out of the city of Nazareth into Judea, into

the city of David, which is called Bethlehem, to be taxed with Mary, his espoused wife.

Song.   We welcome the beautiful Christmas time,
             Its carols of joy we sing;
           The bells in our hearts play a joyful chime,
             As jubilant church - bells ring.
           And so the dear story we tell anew,
             And sing as the angels sang,
           When down from the heights of heavenly blue
             The carols of Christmas rang.
Chorus. Come, seraph choir, and sing with us again
           The song of peace on earth, good will to men.

Recitation. And she brought forth her first-born Son, and wrapped Him in swaddling clothes, and laid Him in a manger, because there was no room for them in the inn.

Song.   No room in the houses of Bethlehem;
             No room in the inn, they say;
           So Mary and Joseph, shut out from them.
             The babe in the manger lay.
           Oh, city of David, no longer thou
             The least in the land shalt dwell,
           For out of thee cometh a ruler now
             To rule over Israel.

Recitation. And there were in the same country shepherds, abiding in the field, keeping watch over their flocks by night.

Song.   While tending the fold in the field by night—
             Oh, what did the shepherds hear?
           An angel of God, with a glorious light,
             Came, bidding them not to fear.
           And, suddenly, hosts of the angels then
             Came down from the starry sky,
           On earth, singing peace and good will to men,
             And glory to God on high.

Recitation. And it came to pass, as the angels were gone away from them into heaven, the shepherds said, one to another:

Song.   " We 'll go, even now, into Bethlehem,
   And see where the child is laid."
  Away when the angels had gone from them
   The wondering shepherds said.
  They, when they had seen it, made known abroad
   The tidings of joy; and then
  The shepherds, rejoicing and praising God,
   Returned to their flocks again.

Recitation. Now, when Jesus was born in Bethlehem of Judea,
there came wise men from the East to Jerusalem.

Song.   The wise men came seeking, from lands afar,
   The King of the Jews, they said;
  And lo! in the heavens a shining star
   Its light o 'er the manger shed.
  There Mary they found, and behold with her
   The wonderful first - born son!
  And treasures of incense, gold, and myrrh,
   They gave to the kingly one!

Recitation. And the shepherds returned, glorifying and praising
God. And the wise men departed into their own country.

Song.   No longer the star in the Eastern sky
   Leads down as it led of old!—
  The shepherds keep watch in the fields on high,
   O 'er lambs of the upper fold!
  The glory that shone over them by night,
   Now shines over us by day;
  We seek not the Lord by starry light,
   We 've found Him, the Light! the Way!

In Concert.
He shall be great, and shall be called the Son of the Highest!
And the Lord God shall give unto him the throne of his father David,
And he shall reign over the house of Jacob forever;
And of his kingdom there shall be no end!

The Birth of Jesus.

Words by M. B. C. SLADE.   Music by GEO. F. ROOT.

Joyfully.

We wel-come the beau-ti - ful Christ - mas time, Its

car - ols of joy we sing ; The bells in our hearts play a

joy - ful chime, As ju - bi - lant church-bells ring : And

so the dear sto - ry we tell a - new, And

THE BIRTH OF JESUS---*concluded.*

sing as the an-gels sang. When down from the heights of the

heav'n - ly blue, The car - ols of Christ-mas rang.

CHORUS.

Come, ser - aph choir, and sing with us a - gain

The song of peace on earth, good will to men.

CHRISTMAS PANTOMIME.

BY MINNIE B. SLADE.

CHARACTERS:

FATHER.	SANTA CLAUS.
MOTHER.	CHILDREN—NANNIE AND NED.
SALESMAN.	SERVANT.

COSTUMES:

Children—Night-dresses. *Santa Claus*—Coat trimmed with fur, fur hat, large bag, filled with toys, on his back. *For the others*— Ordinary dress.

SCENE. I. A toy and confectionery store, with shopman behind counter; various toys on the counter and floor. Enter, father and mother, who look around at toys. They seem to ask to see others. Shopman shows a large doll. They ask price; shake their heads, seeming to say, "too high"; question it. Shopman shows a smaller one; suits better. They buy it, and other toys. Father counts out the money; waits for change. As he turns, sees rocking-horse and drum; touches the latter; mother raises her hands, shakes her head, puts hands to ears; father insists, and buys it. Then buys oranges, candy, etc.; pays again, and they pass out, salesman bowing and promising to send things.

SCENE II. A sitting-room. Bell rings. In a moment servant enters, and brings rocking-horse, drum, doll, and large toys, with various bundles; leaves them on the table and floor. Santa Claus appears at the door; looks in; sees no one; comes and carefully takes things and hides them outside, and disappears. Parents enter; seem amazed. Mother calls servant; asks where the toys are. Servant does n't know. Father accuses her of having taken them. She denies. Father and mother still perplexed. Curtain falls.

SCENE III. Chamber with fire-place, in which burns a wood fire. *This can be easily made by simply painting a fire-place on a paper fire-board.* Arrange so that Santa Claus can, without its being noticeable, move it aside enough to come in between it and the curtain forming the back of the room. As the curtain rises, the little children are sitting on the floor before the fire, talking busily; their clothes on chairs near by. They ask, " Where is Santa Claus?" apparently calling up the chimney to him. They run to the chairs and get each a stocking; hold it up; find it too small. Ned finds a hole in his; shakes his head; shows it to Nannie. She starts, and seems to tell him that she will get a better one; runs out and returns with two very large blue yarn stockings. They laugh, but as they go to hang them up, seem to question as to how Santa Claus can tell them apart. Run to table and write their names, which they pin on the tops, and then hang a stocking on each side of fireplace. Get into bed. Then, in a moment, Santa Claus puts his head in at the fire-place, making a slight noise, which wakes the children, who jump up and look at him; and then, as he goes back, look in their stockings; but finding nothing, seeming very disappointed, go back to bed. Santa Claus returns, and this time comes in; goes to the bed, sees children asleep, and then fills stockings, commenting, apparently, at each article. He drums a noiseless march, and puts the sticks in, and drum under stocking; blows the trumpet, and at the sound, starts, and turns to the bed to see if he has waked the children; turns back to his toys; seems to rock the doll in his arms, and puts her head-first into Ned's stocking; finds his mistake, and corrects it; puts cradle under stocking, and then piles in and around the stockings bundles, smaller toys, oranges, candy, and the like. Starts to go up the chimney, and, seeming to have just remembered, goes to door, and carefully draws in a rocking-horse, which he leaves by the bed-side. Then standing by the children, he seems to shout, " Merry Christmas! " to them, and turns, and disappears up chimney, and rides off in his sleigh. The bells ringing loudly, wake the children, who run to the stockings, exclaiming at each article, drumming, blowing trumpet, trying on mittens, rocking doll in cradle, eating candy, rocking on horse, and having general merriment. They seem to shout, "Thank you!" to Santa Claus, up the chimney, and while their play continues, curtain falls.

CHRISTMAS GIFTS — OR, WHAT WE DO AT OUR HOUSE.

FOR FOUR LITTLE GIRLS.

BY MARY B. C. SLADE.

First Girl. What do you do at your house, when Christmas eve is
nigh?

Second Girl. We stretch a line at the chimney-side,
And mother sees it is strongly tied;
Then, hang our stockings, and go to bed.
And just as soon as our prayer is said,
We wonder and guess, till asleep we fall,
What Santa Claus has for one and all.
Then, long before daylight, we haste to pull
From the line by the chimney our stockings full.
    And that's what we do at our house.
What do you do at your house when Christmas eve is
nigh?

Third Girl. We have in the parlor a Christmas tree;
And each has his own little mystery
In hanging upon the branches green
His gifts for the others, by them unseen.
Then mother goes in, the candles to light,
And everything is so gay and bright,
That you ought to be there, our joy to see,
When we have our gifts from the Christmas tree;
    And that's what we do at our house.
What do you do at your house when Christmas eve is
nigh?

Fourth Girl. We hear in the evening a rousing ring;
We hurry the door to open fling;
And, sure as you live, with his long white hair,
And his jolly red face, Santa Claus is there!
He opens his pack, and, with laugh and shout,
We take the presents he tosses about.
Then he's off; but just after his visit is o'er,
Uncle John comes in at the other door!
    And that's what we do at our house.
What do you do at your house when Christmas eve is
nigh?

First Girl. We, too, hang our stockings; but mother says,
One thing we must do — all Christmas days —
Just as sure as they come, just as long as we live;
Some gifts to the poor we must always give.
So a basket she fills, on Christmas eve,
And tells us just where our gifts to leave.
Would you know how the best time at Christmas is
found?
Help Santa Claus carry his basket around;
For that's what we do at our house.

WELCOME.

BY THE VERY SMALLEST BOY.

Bowing. I'm going to speak the welcome : all you men and boys,
I'm very glad you've come ; but you must n't make any
noise !
They told me to make a bow, and not be afraid of the
men.
Who's afraid! I've made it once, now I'll make it again!
Bows, and runs off the stage.

A very little girl runs on.

He did n't welcome the ladies ! What a funny fellow !—
Pointing to audience.
Oh, what a pretty bonnet, trimmed with blue and yellow!
But you must n't be looking 'round ; look right straight
at me !
Ladies and girls, you are welcome — just as welcome as
can be !
And the men and boys are welcome, just as much, and
just the same ;
I hope every one of you, when you go home, will say you
are glad you came !

A CHRISTMAS DIALOGUE.

FOR SEVEN LITTLE GIRLS.

BY M. B. C. SLADE.

Mary. I 've been thinking, little sisters, if a heathen child should
  be
Hither brought from some lone islet in the far-off southern
  sea,
And should ask why summer garlands deck our house
  this wintry day,
Why we seem so glad and happy, Annie dear, what
  would you say ?

Annie. I would tell the lovely story of the Babe of Bethlehem ;
How they laid Him in the manger, when by night He came
  to them ;
I would tell how Mary dressed Him, and, with soft and
  fragrant hay,
I think the manger-bed she made, where baby Jesus lay.

Fanny. I would tell that gentle shepherds, watching o'er their
  flocks by night,
Saw, suddenly around them, the shining glory-light,
And heard the angel's tidings about a Savior's birth,
And then the heavenly chorus, "Good will and peace on
  earth."

Bessie. I 'd tell the wondrous story about the guiding-star,
That led the holy wise men from eastern lands afar,
Until they found sweet Mary, and Jesus-child with her,
And gave Him precious presents—gold, frankincense and
  myrrh.

Carrie. Then I would tell how Jesus, this little, blessed child,
Grew up to perfect manhood, holy, pure, and undefiled ;
How, living, serving, dying, Himself for us He gave—
He loved us so he lived and died, our souls from sin to
  save.

Nettie. Then to the little heathen child I think that I would say,
  " Do n't you think that we have shown you why we love
  the Christmas day ?

Do n't you see we must be happy, and our happy gladness show,

Upon the birthday of the One who blessed and loved us so ? "

Susie. And then we all would promise the heathen child that we Would send the knowledge of His love to islands of the sea.

Till all the world shall Christmas keep, rejoicing for His birth,

At which the shining angels sang, "Good will and peace on earth."

From "Pure Diamonds." By permission.

CAST YOUR NETS ON THE OTHER SIDE!

RECITE JOHN, XXI: 3-6.

BY MARY B. C. SLADE.

Seven fishers went out by night at sea,
In a ship on the waves of Galilee;
In vain they toiled till the night was o'er,
Then Jesus stood on the shining shore;
Across the sound of the sea he cried:
" Cast your nets on the other side!"—
The other side, the other side!
  Ye shall fill your nets on the other side!

Not one of the seven said, " Why, Oh, Lord ? "
For they loved to obey the Master's word.
They cast, therefore, and behold they saw
Their nets more full than their hands could draw!
They then rejoiced that the dear Lord cried,
" Cast your nets on the other side !"—
The other side, the other side!
  Ye shall fill your nets on the other side!

Ye fishers who go as fishers of men,
Casting over your nets all night in vain,
The long dark hours have ye toiled within
The tossing waves of a sea of sin!

Your Master calls at the morning tide,
" Cast your nets on *the other side !* "—
The other side, the other side!
Ye shall fill your nets on the other side!

O, brothers! be glad, and strong in the faith;
Ye are fishers of men, the Master saith;
And grow not faint, though the toil seem vain,
But cast your nets to the right again.
The dear Lord's voice in your heart shall guide;
" Cast your nets on the other side! "— .
The other side, the other side!
Ye shall fill your nets on *the other side !*

[The above may be found, *with music* by Emilius Laroche, in J. R. Murray's
" Pure Diamonds," published by Brainard's Sons, Cleveland, Ohio.]

SIX "BETHS."
A RECITATION FOR SEVEN LITTLE GIRLS.

BY M. B. C. SLADE.

First Girl. What Scripture names have you all learned well?
Six in Concert. Names begining with *Beth*, we show,
First Girl. What does that mean, can you all now tell?
Six Girls. *The house of*, or *place of* — that we know.
Second Girl. Bethel is the place where Jacob dreamed
Of the beautiful ladder; where angels seemed
To ascend and descend from the skies;—said he,
" This place is the *House of God*, for me!"

Jacob said, " This is none other but the house of God." * * *
"And he called the name of that place Bethel."—Gen. xxviii:
17, 19.

Third Girl. The *place of dates*, where grew the palm,
Was Bethany, quiet, peaceful, calm.
Where often, at eventide, Jesus loved best
With Lazarus, Martha and Mary to rest.

"And now the eventide was come, he went out unto Bethany with
the twelve."— Mark, xi: 11.

Fourth Girl.   *Place of mercy,* Bethesda, the sweet, tender name
    Of the waters where Jesus once raised up the lame.
    No need for an angel, the waters to move,
    When Jesus drew nigh, full of pity and love.

" There is at Jerusalem a pool which is called, in the Hebrew
tongue, Bethesda, having five porches."— John, v: 2.

Fifth Girl.   Bethphage, the *place of figs,* my place once meant,
    Where Jesus remained, and his two servants sent,
    Saying, " Go to the village, a colt you shall see
    Whereon never man sat; loose him, bring him to me."

"And it came to pass when he was come nigh unto Bethphage
* * * he sent two of his disciples, saying, * * * ye shall
find a colt whereon never man sat; loose him and bring him to
me."— Luke, xix: 29, 30.

Sixth Girl.   My place is Bethabara, *place of the ford,*
    Where John came preparing the way of the Lord;
    Where he was baptizing, when Pharisees came
    To ask him, "Who art thou, and what is thy name?"

" These things were done in Bethabara, beyond Jordan, where
John was baptizing."— John, i: 28.

Seventh Girl.   My *Beth* is the dearest and best of them,
    For *The House of Bread,* it is Bethlehem,
    Where Jesus was born, when the angels of light
    Sang to shepherds that watched their flocks by night.

"And it came to pass as the angels were gone away from them
into heaven, the shepherds said, one to another, Let us go, even
now, unto Bethlehem, and see this thing which has come to pass."
—Luke, ii: 18.

First Girl.   Now, can you repeat these names with me,
    And remember the meaning of them?

Six in Concert. Bethel, Bethany, Bethabara, Bethphage,
    Bethesda, and Bethlehem.

THE OBEDIENCE OF JESUS.

BY MARY B. C. SLADE.

The dearest picture of our Lord
    Is where the Scripture saith,
He subject was to Mary's word,
    In lowly Nazareth.
The grace of God was on Him when
    He strong in spirit grew ;
Yet He obeyed His parents, then,
    Was subject them unto.

They found Him at Jerusalem,
    Among the doctors wise,
Both questioning and giving them
    Astonishing replies.
His Father's business He knows,
    His work He has begun ;
Yet down to Nazareth He goes,
    A faithful, subject Son.

Oh, young child Jesus, wise and strong,
    And full of God's dear grace,
From Thee I learn what ways belong
    To childhood's time and place.
This picture will I keep of Thee,
    The word the Scripture saith,
And subject to my parents be,
    As Thou, at Nazareth.

• • •

THE CARE OF JESUS.

BY MARY B. C. SLADE.

Upon the cruel cross of woe,
    Hung Jesus, crucified!
His weeping mother, down below,
    Stood close the cross beside.

The waves of anguish o'er Him roll,
Her Babe, her Son, her Lord ;
And Mary's silent, suff'ring soul,
Is pierced with sorrow's sword.

And that disciple, he could see,
The best-beloved one ;
" Behold thy mother ! " then said he ;
" Woman, behold thy Son ! "
And from that hour, to his own home,
He who on Jesus' breast
Was wont to lean, bade Mary come,
And in its shelter rest.

O, love divine, that, stooping down
From crucifixion's woe,
Could kindly care for these, His own,
Because He loved them so.
May we, in sorrow, pain, or loss,
For others' good provide,
As for Thy mother, at the cross,
Didst Thou, the crucified.

GLIMPSES OF JESUS.

BY M. B. C. SLADE.

I.

First Voice.	Who is this upon Nazareth's hills, Gathering lilies that grow by the rills ?
All.	Jesus of Nazareth ; from Jerusalem He came with his parents—was subject unto them.

II.

Second Voice.	Who is this in the Bethany home, Where He so tenderly loved to come ?
All.	Jesus of Nazareth. Low at His feet Mary is learning her lessons sweet.

III.

Third Voice.   Who is this, where the waters cool,
                 Gleam as they flow from Siloam's pool ?

All.   Jesus of Nazareth, tender, kind,
                 Stands by Siloam and heals the blind.

IV.

Fourth Voice. Who is this, in the eventide,
                 Walking up slowly o'er Olive's side ?

All.   Jesus of Nazareth goes that way :
                 Thither he comes by night to pray.

V.

Fifth Voice.   Who is this, by the blue sea's shore,
                 Watching the waves when the night is o'er ?

All.   Jesus of Nazareth ; it is He,
                 Waiting His fisher friends to see.

VI.

Sixth Voice.   Who has come, at the ruler's cries,
                 Bidding his little daughter rise ?

All.   Jesus of Nazareth ; and he said,
                 " Maiden, arise ! " " She is not dead ! "

VII.

Seventh Voice. Who is this, when the mothers press
                 Near Him, that He their babes may bless ?

All.   Jesus of Nazareth ; kindly He
                 Says, " Let the little ones come to me."

VIII.

Eighth Voice. Sweetly our glimpses of Jesus fall ;
                 This is the dearest one of all.

All.   Jesus of Nazareth, let me be
                 One of the children blessed by Thee.

WHAT DECEMBER SAYS.

A CHRISTMAS RECITATION.

BY MARY B. C. SLADE.

Open your hearts, ere I am flown,
  And hear my old, old story;
For I am the month that first looked down
  On the beautiful Babe of glory.
You never must call me lone and drear,
  Because no birds are singing;
Open your hearts and you shall hear
  The song of the angels ringing.

Open your hearts and hear the feet
  Of the star-led wise men olden;
Bring out your treasures of incense sweet;
  Lay down your offerings golden.
You say you look, but you see no sight
  Of the wonderful Babe I'm telling;
You say they have carried Him off by night,
  From Bethlehem's lowly dwelling.

Open your hearts, and seek the door,
  Where the alway-poor are staying.
For this is the story, forevermore,
  The Master's voice is saying:
Inasmuch as ye do it unto them,
  The poor, the weak, and the stranger,
Ye do it to Jesus of Bethlehem,
  The Babe of the star-lit manger.

A LITTLE SERMON, FOR A LITTLE BOY.

BY MARY B. C. SLADE.

I 'm but a little fellow, to stand up here and preach.
My sermon is to teachers, who little children teach:
Habbakuk ii: 2, my subject will contain.
"MAKE IT PLAIN:" that is my text; *Make it plain; make it plain;*

Firstly: Small boys and girls do n't know very much;
When you teach the Scripture, make it plain to such.
Secondly: I will illustrate, just as the preachers do,
By telling you an anecdote—my hearers, it is true:
A very little girl, in Sunday school had learned
The story that Lot's wife to a pillar of salt was turned.
Now what a pillar was, this child she did not know;
And in her little mind she thought 't was a *pillow !*
So she gravely asked, one day (and it was not her fault),
If Lot's wife, in the resurrection, would rise *a bag of salt !*
Thirdly : If that child's teacher had shown what pillars were,
Do n't you see it had been easy to make it plain to her?
Fourthly, and last, in closing, I'll give my text again:
Habbakuk ii: 2.   *Make it plain; make it plain.*

A LITTLE THING.

BY MARY B. C. SLADE.

Once, in Judea's holy earth,
A sapling sprang : its humble birth
      Was meek and low :
            It grew not on
            Proud Lebanon,
      But where sweet Kedron's pleasant waters flow.

Spring's mild, soft showers, and summer's heat,
Nursed the young plant ; and at its feet
            An offering
            Bright Kedron threw ;
            And so it grew
      A stately tree—that very little thing.

Oh, sad the change, and hard to tell,
That o'er the tree of beauty fell;
            Struck to the ground,
            Its branches wide
            Kissed Kedron's side,
      And chill winds swept its withered leaves around.

So low it lay, the passers by
Gazed on it with a pitying eye,
And mourned its loss.
Oh, should those eyes
Behold it rise,
That fallen tree, a suffering Savior's cross !

A little thing they called it, when
It budded first ; oh, shall we, then,
Mere trifles call
Life's little things,
When time thus brings
The greatest ends from such beginnings small ?

THE PARABLE OF THE TREES.

SCRIPTURE RECITATION.

The trees went forth, on a time, to anoint a King over them; and they said unto the olive tree, "Reign thou over us."

But the olive tree said unto them, "Should I leave my fatness, wherewith by me they honor God and man, and go to be promoted over the trees ?"

And the trees said to the fig tree, "Come thou, and reign over us."

But the fig tree said unto them, "Should I forsake my sweetness and good fruits, and go to be promoted over the trees ?"

Then said the trees unto the vine, "Come thou and reign over us."

And the vine said unto them, "Should I leave my wine, which cheereth God and man, and go to be promoted over the trees ?"

Then said all the trees unto the bramble, "Come thou and reign over us."

And the bramble said unto the trees, "If in truth ye anoint me King over you, then come and put your trust in my shadow; and if not, let fire come out of the bramble and devour the cedars of Lebanon."

AT THE CHRISTMAS TREE.

RECITATION FOR BOY OR GIRL.

BY MARY B. C. SLADE.

Some love the oak tree, tall and strong ;
 The willow, bending down ;
The elm, with graceful branches long ;
 The pine, with sweet, sad song ;
The cherry tree, whose petals white
 Fall soft as summer's snow ;
The apple tree, with blossoms bright,
 And fruit of golden glow.
But this strange tree, our favorite,
 Through one glad hour shall be ;
For love's dear blossoms cover it —
 It is our Christmas tree.
Around the tree we stand to-night,
 And joyfully declare,
Some lovely fruit, or blossoms bright,
 For each, its branches bear.
His sun and rain our Father lends
 To deck the forest trees;
His love in human hearts he sends
 To make such bloom as these.
So, while we bless these hands of love
 That Christmas gifts bestow,
We'll thank the tender Heart above,
 Whence all our blessings flow.

www.ingramcontent.com/pod-product-compliance
Lightning Source LLC
Chambersburg PA
CBHW021639270326
41931CB00008B/1088